Falling in Love with You

OTHER BOOKS
BY MARY O'MALLEY

The Magical Forest of Aliveness:
A Tale of Awakening

Belonging to Life:
The Journey of Awakening

The Gift of Our Compulsions:
A Revolutionary Approach to Self-Acceptance and Healing

What's in the Way Is the Way:
A Practical Guide for Waking Up to Life

For more information about Mary O'Malley and her offerings,
please visit www.maryomalley.com

FALLING IN LOVE WITH YOU

Nuggets of wisdom
for a heartfelt life

Mary O'Malley

Awakening
WITH MARY O'MALLEY

Cover design and book interior by Maureen Gately, www.gatelystudio.com
Edited by Devrah Bennett

ISBN: (Trade Paperback) 979-8-5544629-6-2

ISBN: (e-Book) 978-0-9720848-9-5

Manufactured in the United States of America
10 9 8 7 6 5 4 3 2 1

Keywords: oneness, presence, meditation, spirituality, inspiration, insight, self-love, self-help, compassion, mindfulness, healing, personal growth, love, self-acceptance, higher-consciousness, awakening

This book is dedicated to my children,
Katrina and Micah who, as they were growing up,
showed me how to love myself exactly as I am.

FOREWORD

By Neale Donald Walsch,
author of *Conversations with God*

ONE OF THE BIGGEST CHALLENGES OF LIFE, in my experience, is to love oneself. I mean completely, absolutely, unconditionally, without qualification or hesitation. Most people I have talked to about this (including myself, in the mirror) so often see in ourselves imperfection after imperfection, giving us reason upon reason to judge ourselves, to demean ourselves, and to feel unworthy of being honored by others for anything we have done, or loved by others for the way they think we are. I refer to this as the Imposter Syndrome, a state of mind into which we can fall far too easily and too often, in which we imagine ourselves to be putting on an "act" that shows us to be better or other than what and how we really are.

The truth is that, for nearly every person, the opposite is true. We are nicer, kinder, more understanding, compassionate, courageous, generous, and loving than we give ourselves credit for being. It is we who we've been fooling into thinking that we are less than we are. For many this is the result of coming of age in a culture or religion (or both) which told us that we are not good enough and must not think of ourselves as special in any way. But now along comes marvelous, magical, mystical teacher Mary O'Malley to disabuse us of all those notions.

Here, in a collection of conveniently brief but wonderfully illuminating insights from the heart of what she offers to the world, are eye-opening, mind-opening, heart-opening morsels to feed the part of all of us that has, more than once, starved for permission to think well of ourselves. All we have ever needed was some encouragement along the way. This is it. Now we can give even more magnificently to others, as we embrace a full awareness of the wonder of who we are.

But wait. Is it truly okay for you to fall in love with you? And can it be done? Really? Can all the old training be overcome?

Turn the page and see.

In this never to be repeated moment,

in the vastness of all time and space,

you have been given

the miraculous gift of life.

In the universal scheme of things,

you are a tiny, tiny expression of life

but also, and most importantly,

you are completely unique

and totally necessary.

There has never been anybody like you
and there never will be.
Life created you
because it needed you.

One of the core assignments
you have been given by life
is to fall deeply and completely in love
with you exactly *as you are*.

And yet

you have been on a long, long journey

away from the wisdom of your heart,

away from meeting yourself

with the healing balm of insight

and compassion.

So have we all!

As you were growing up, like all of us,

you learned to be what you felt

the people around you needed you to be

in order to receive the attention necessary

for survival. You buried the so-called

unacceptable parts of you deep inside,

so deep that now you are rarely aware

they are there.

Focusing on what you should be, you

learned to judge, second guess, distrust,

deny and even hate yourself.

Such deep pain we all carry!

Most of us have been conditioned

with the illusion of needing to be perfect,

spending our lives trying to live up

to what we think we should be,

and so many times

feeling we are falling short.

'Persona', the root of the word

personality, means mask.

We are all wearing masks, trying to be cool,

trying to be accepted. It takes a lot of trust

in another to let down your mask.

So be willing to let it down with yourself.

It is okay to be you.

These words you are reading
are an invitation to come back home
to your heart,
discovering how to loosen
and eventually dissolve the beliefs
you took on, which say
you are not worthy of love,
especially your own love.

"You can search
throughout the entire universe
for someone more deserving
of your love and affection
than you are yourself,
and that person
is not to be found anywhere.
You, yourself, as much as anybody
in the entire universe,
deserve your love and affection."

Buddha

It is your birthright

to love and accept yourself as you are.

This doesn't mean that you don't try

bettering yourself.

It just means your healing doesn't arise

from the belief that you are not okay.

The depth of love you are ready for
doesn't require another human being
although it is wonderful
to share love with others.

Instead, it is a love that is discovered
by opening into a caring, friendly,
trusting, and respectful relationship
with yourself.

"The best and most beautiful things
in this world cannot be seen
or even heard
but must be felt with the heart."

HELEN KELLER

The greatest gift

you can give to yourself and others

is to fall in love with yourself

exactly as you are.

Is this easy?

No!

But it is totally possible!

"In the temple
of your own body,
within your heart
is a lotus flower.
Within the lotus
is an illuminated
jewel space.
Find who dwells
in this precious space
within your heart.
Know that person,
love that being.
That is you!"

Chandogya Upanishad

The person
who most deserves kindness is you!

♥

The person you most deeply want
to receive kindness from
is you.

You are the only person
you wake up with every morning
and you are the only person
you go to bed with every single night.
And nobody can love you
as fully and completely
as you can love you!

If you saw you as God sees you,
you would smile a lot.

NEALE DONALD WALSCH

In order to fall in love with you,
it is important to know you are not alone
in the struggles you have experienced:

We all have been hurt and are afraid
of being hurt again.

We all have had moments
and possibly even days and years
when life was just too much.

We all have been judged, sometimes unmercifully,
and we have all judged others.

We all have felt inadequate
around a particular task
and sometimes even for life.

We all have felt foolish, embarrassed and inept,
and wish fervently nobody ever sees us
in those states.

We all can be truly unmerciful with ourselves.

We all experience the feeling of being unseen,
unheard and not valued.

We all have known an undercurrent of unease,
which we don't want to acknowledge.
And we have all known the kind of fear
that makes it hard to breathe.

We all are deeply afraid
that other people will see
what is truly going on inside of us,
sure that if they do, we will be rejected and alone.

We are also afraid of seeing
what is going on inside of us,
causing us to keep overly busy
rather than opening to what we are experiencing
in this moment, and meeting it
with our accepting attention.

We all abandon ourselves
when we most need ourselves.

We are all struggling.
And we all long to have our hearts open again,
loving ourselves as we are,
present for the astounding beauty
and mystery of life.

"Perhaps
everything that frightens us is,
in its deepest essence,
something helpless
that wants *our* love."

Rainer Maria Rilke,

Letters to a Young Poet

"For today,
treat yourself
as if you
were your only
child."

Stephen Levine

Living from your heart
does not weaken you
as some people believe.
In fact, it makes you stronger.

It is not selfish to care for you.
In fact, it is self-full.

You

♥

deserve

♥

your

♥

love!

You may say other people
deserve to come home to their heart,
but you don't.
This just isn't true.
There is not one person
in the whole world who doesn't
deserve to feel the healing warmth
of their own heart
and this includes you.

Pause for a moment
and place your hand over your heart,
feeling as much tenderness for yourself
as you can.
If your mind resisted doing this,
recognize it as an opportunity
to see how challenging it can be
to meet yourself with kindness.

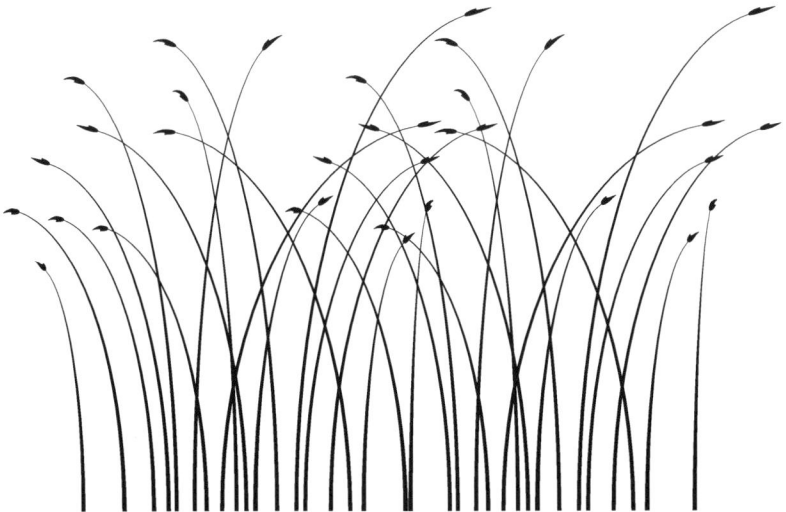

"A moment of self-compassion
can change your entire day.
A string of such moments can change
the course of your life."

CHRISTOPHER K. GERMER

Trying to fix, change or understand
may sometimes be necessary,
but it isn't where lasting healing
happens. All deep healing happens
in the presence of your accepting,
enfolding heart.

"When I started loving myself,
I recognized, that my thinking can
make me miserable and sick.
When I requested for my heart forces,
my mind got an important partner.
Today I call this connection
HEART WISDOM."

CHARLIE CHAPLIN

Are you ready to live beyond
the tight and small space of your mind
and instead live from the spaciousness,
nourishment and wisdom
of your heart?

Living from your heart
allows you to discover it is safe
to be naturally you.
Then your belly softens,
your breath opens,
and you connect again
with the joy of
simply being!

Kindness, care, compassion,

and love

all come from your heart.

So too does your courage,

strength, clarity,

and the passion to be fully alive.

Fall deeply and completely
in love with you
so you can joyfully dance
and sing in your own parade!

"Science is validating
what humans have known
throughout the ages:
that compassion is not a luxury;
it is a necessity for our well-being,
resilience, and survival."

Joan Halifax

The more you fall in love with you,

the more the quiet whispers

of your wise heart become louder

than the voices in your head.

Having one of those days
where life really sucks,
we rarely think about being
kind to ourselves. And yet
just a few moments of self-kindness
will change the trajectory of your day.

Your heart will tell you that you are perfectly imperfect. You are beautifully flawed. Your perfection includes your imperfections!

There is nothing wrong with you!
You, like all of us, are a mixture
of dark and light!
Always have been
and always will be!

You will be a work in progress
until your last breath.
There is no such thing as getting it all
together and there is no such thing
as a 'perfect' person.

"It is with the heart
that one sees rightly.
What is essential is invisible to the eye
(the mind)."

THE LITTLE PRINCE

As you fall in love with yourself,
you will see that deep inside
there are parts of you that are scared, angry,
afraid and lonely,
and believe you need to be better
or different than who you are
in order to be loved.
You are not alone
in having these feelings.
We all have them and yet
try to hide them from ourselves
and others.

"Your task is not to seek for love,
but merely to seek and find
all the barriers within yourself
that you have built against it."

RUMI

The more you fall in love with you,

frustration, resistance, anxiety, fury,

despair, loneliness, grief, irritation

(to name a few) will awaken

your heart rather than getting you lost

in your busy and reactive mind

so you can meet yourself

with the compassion you deserve.

You can have compassion
for yourself even in your deepest
and darkest times.
Place your hand over your heart
and take a few moments
to breathe in compassion
and then shower yourself
with its nectar on your out-breath.

"That I feed the hungry,

forgive an insult,

love my enemy, these are great virtues.

But what if I should discover

that the poorest of the beggars

and the most impudent of offenders

are all within me,

and that I stand in need of the alms

of my own kindness?

What happens then?"

CARL JUNG

Embracing every single part
of yourself with the wisdom
and kindness of your heart,
makes it safe for you to become
authentically you.

"In my humble view,
the most 'awake' ones are the ones
who have cultivated a deep,
warm compassion within,
a profound self-kindness
and who radiate that delicious
empathy into the world."

JEFF FOSTER

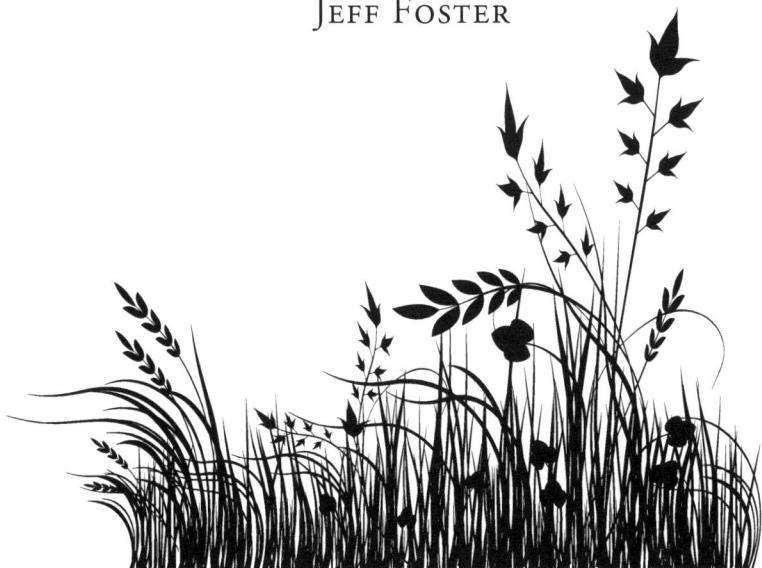

Are you ready to fall in love
with that which you have formally
hated, resisted and feared
about yourself? Are you ready
to fall in love with all of you?
If you said no, be compassionate
with the part of you that is still afraid
of meeting yourself as you are.
Remember, everybody else has
the same parts,
which you may still be ashamed of
and afraid of.

As you heal the struggles
in your mind, which are always trying
to make something happen
or get to someplace better,
you discover that you can be
with whatever you are experiencing,
even if it is something you formerly
feared like loss, fury, despair, illness,
loneliness or death.

"When your heart at last acknowledges
how much pain there is in your mind,
it turns like a mother
toward a frightened child."

STEPHEN LEVINE

The more you fall in love with you,
you will no longer need to prove
that you are enough
for *you know you are enough*
—exactly as you are.

We have all done unskillful things
to ourselves and others.
We have all made mistakes we don't
want anybody to know about.
We've all had thoughts and feelings
we feel we must hide
from ourselves and others.
This doesn't make you bad or wrong.
It just means you are human.

For a few moments
let go of "I should have done this"
or "I shouldn't of done that"
or "Nobody else does this as much
as I do" or "Everybody else
does it better than I do."
Instead let the healing balm
of self-acceptance fill you
with its deep and abiding
nourishment.

We are all beautiful
and essentially flawed human beings.
As Elisabeth Kubler-Ross says,
"I'm not okay, you're not okay
and that's okay!"

If you think it is not okay
to have so-called bad thoughts
and feelings,
you will bury these feelings,
but this doesn't make them go away.
In fact, they will come out of hiding
at the most inopportune times.

"The healing is to let yourself in
when you find yourself the most
unacceptable."

STEPHEN LEVINE

There is nothing inside of you
to be ashamed of
or afraid of.

"No better you than the you that you are

No better life than the life we're living

No better time for your shine, you're a star.

Oh, you're beautiful, oh, you're beautiful.

But there's a hope that's waiting for you

in the dark

You should know you're beautiful

just the way you are

And you don't have to change a thing,

the world could change its heart

No scars to your beautiful, we're stars

and we're beautiful."

LYRICS TO *SCARS TO YOUR BEAUTIFUL*

BY ALESSIA CARA

All the so-called
unacceptable thoughts
and feelings inside of you
have been silently requesting,
your whole life, for you to see them
through the light of your accepting
attention.

"Compassion
isn't some kind of self-improvement
project or ideal that we're trying
to live up too.
Having compassion starts and ends
with having compassion
for all those unwanted parts
of ourselves, all those imperfections
that we don't even want to look at."

Pema Chödrön

It is okay to feel/think
what you feel/think.
This is not permission to act
upon your thoughts and feelings.
Instead, it is an invitation
not to struggle with them
so you can bring them the healing light
of your own accepting attention.

"You know quite well,

deep within you,

that there is only a single magic,

a single power, a single salvation. . . .

and that is called loving.

Well, then love your suffering.

Do not resist it, do not flee from it,

it is your aversion that hurts,

nothing else."

HERMANN HESSE

Everything you dislike about yourself
not only deserves
your compassion and understanding
but they hunger for it.

True compassion
means keeping company
with whatever you are experiencing.

True kindness means befriending
whatever you are experiencing.

Be kind
to the parts
inside of you
who struggle.

"If your compassion
does not include yourself,
it is incomplete."

BUDDHA

The more you fall in love with you,

exactly as you are,

criticism of yourself and others

will become much less interesting.

That self-critical voice inside of you
never sees the whole truth.
It adds two and two together
and comes up with 44.

"The greatest barrier to our own healing
is not the pain, sorrow or violence
inflicted upon us as children. Our
greatest hindrance is our ongoing
capacity to judge, to criticize, and to
bring tremendous harm to ourselves.
If we can harden our hearts against
ourselves and meet our most tender
feelings with anger and condemnation,
we simultaneously armor out hearts
against the possibility of gentleness,
love and healing."

WAYNE MULLER

It is okay to make mistakes.

In fact, it is a part of being human.

Rather than judging your mistakes,

learn from them

for they are your teachers.

We are each unique expressions of life, so the truth is . . . there is nobody better than you but also there is nobody less than you.

Be fascinated with what your mind did with this truth.

When you have understanding and
compassion for your unskillful ways
of trying to take care of yourself,
the more these behaviors will fall away.
The so-called nourishment, which
formerly came from overeating,
cigarettes, drugs, busyness, shopping,
etc. now pales in comparison with
the love and care you have for yourself.

"Self-love
is the source
of all our other
loves."

PIERRE CORNIELLE

If you want to know a simple
but profound way to heal,
whatever you are experiencing,
first touch it with love.

"The most difficult times
for many of us
are the ones we give ourselves."

Pema Chödrön

As you fall in love with you,
you will know how
to live in your body,
tapping into its insight
and intelligence.

Eons ago, even before remembering,
the doorway to my heart slammed
shut—locked, sealed, fettered,
bound and deeply broken.

Slowly, as slowly as a flower appears
out of mystery,

it opened . . . and now my dry and
parched soul blooms in pure joy.

The winds of tenderness now cool
me when I am hot

and warm me when I am cold.

And for this I am oh so grateful.

If you want to care for others,

care for yourself first,

for it all comes from you.

As you fill yourself up with your own

accepting attention,

you have more to give to others.

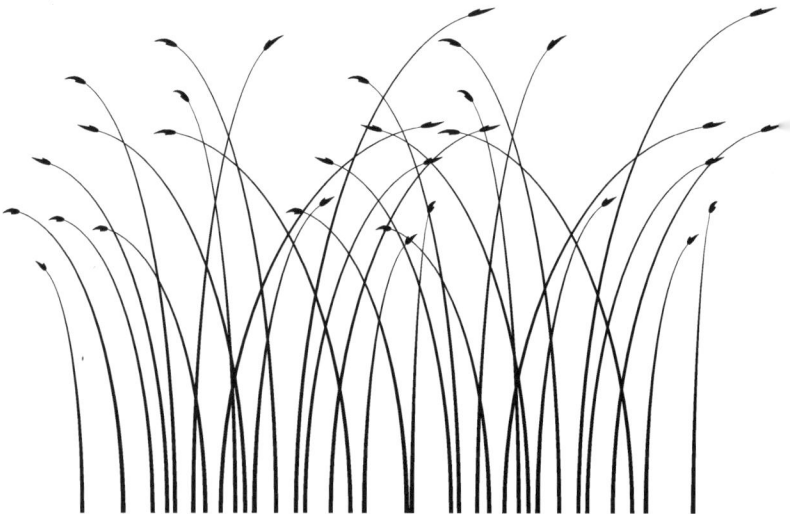

If it feels easier to care for others
than for yourself, imagine
what you would wish for a loved one,
and for today, give it to yourself.

When you are judging somebody,
you are judging a part of you,
which you haven't yet learned
how to accept and love about yourself.

When somebody is judging you,
they are talking about themselves.

The more you fall in love with you,
the more you will be able
to see your friends and loved
ones as simply human—not people
to judge or resist—but people
who deserve understanding
and compassion even though
it may possibly be best not to engage
with them.

"If we could read the secret history
of our enemies, we should find
in each man's life sorrow and suffering enough
to disarm our hostilities."

HENRY WADSWORTH LONGFELLOW

The more you fall in love with you,
the less interested you become
in sharing your thoughts and opinions
because you become more interested
in listening to other people.

The more you live
with love and kindness
for yourself and others,
when meeting someone new,
rather than wondering
what you can get from them,
your focus becomes
what you can give to them.

"The longest journey
you will ever take is the 18 inches
from your head to your heart."

Thích Nhat Hanh

The more you fall in love with you,
you see how precious you are
and also realize how precious
every single person is.

"Our deepest fear
is not that we are inadequate.
Our deepest fear
is that we are powerful
beyond measure.
It is our light not our darkness
that most frightens us.
Your playing small
does not service the world.
There is nothing enlightened
about shrinking so that other people
won't feel insecure around you.
We were all meant to shine
as children do.
It is not just in some of us,
it is in everyone.
And as we let our own light shine,
we unconsciously give other people
permission to do the same.
As we are liberated from our own fear
our presence automatically
liberates others."

MARIANNE WILLIAMSON

The more you open your heart to
yourself, the more you will be able
to cherish every single part of life,
for you no longer see through the lens
of 'them or us'. You will see there is
only one of us here and that includes
animals, insects, plants, rocks, fish,
water, the atmosphere, and of course
people. We are all family, sharing this
beautiful jewel of a planet together.
When you KNOW this, you then
become an instrument of healing
wherever you go.

When you fall in love with you,
everybody and everything you meet
will benefit from your presence.

Aimless Love

This morning as I walked along the lake shore,
I fell in love with a wren
and later in the day with a mouse
the cat had dropped under the dining room table.

In the shadows of an autumn evening,
I fell for a seamstress
still at her machine in the tailor's window,
and later for a bowl of broth,
steam rising like smoke from a naval battle.

This is the best kind of love, I thought,
without recompense, without gifts,
or unkind words, without suspicion,
or silence on the telephone.

BILLY COLLINS

The more you meet yourself
with kindness and compassion,
the noise in your mind quiets down
and you see that you are
so much more than you have thought
yourself to be.

The more you fall in love with you,
the more you see that you
are made out of pure love.

The more you fall in love with you,
the more you see that everything
is made out of love.

Everything is love
or a call for love.

A Course in Miracles

The truth is that every day
you breathe love, you drink love,
you eat love, and you are showered
by love wherever you go.

🦋

You are cared for
more than you can possibly know.

"Love is the reality of realities,
the incomprehensibly glorious
truth of truths that lives and breathes
at the core of everything that exists
or will ever exist."

EBEN ALEXANDER, NEUROSURGEON,

AUTHOR OF *PROOF OF HEAVEN*

And this includes you!

"There is a vitality, a life force,
an energy, a quickening that is
translated into action. And because
there is only one of you in all of time,
this expression is unique. And if you
block it, it will never exist through any
other medium and will be lost. The
world will not have it. It is not your
business to determine how good it is,
nor how valuable, nor how it compares
with other expressions. It is your
business to keep it yours clearly and
directly; to keep the channels open.
You do not even have to believe in
yourself or your work; you have to
keep open and aware directly of the
urges that motivate you."

MARTHA GRAHAM

"How we feel about ourselves
will determine the future of the world.
Whether distraction and aggression
proliferate globally
or peacefulness and harmony
grow stronger
depends on how we,
as citizens of the world,
feel about ourselves."

PEMA CHÖDRÖN

We come full circle. . . .

In the universal scheme of things,

you are a tiny, tiny expression of life

but also, and most importantly,

you are completely unique

and totally necessary.

There has never been anybody like you
and there never will be.

Life created you
because it needed you.

And we need you to be the fullest you,
you can possibly be.

It is possible to totally fall in love with yourself exactly as you are. Actually, it is not only possible; it is absolutely necessary, for our world will be healed as more and more people live from their hearts. So, fall in love with you! It is the most courageous thing you can do!

We need you!

"The desire to make us over into love permeates the whole universe. We are initiated into love when lured into the intense pursuit of the enchanted lover and if the initiation is long and filled with doubt and suffering, the learning takes hold deeply. The slow learner has so many more opportunities to see how shrewd love can be as it penetrates all his character armor. Such stubborn human beings are the world's greatest lovers for they have been through an initiation that demanded many resources of love. They make themselves just as irresistible and intelligent as love in drawing others into the joy of living."

Brian Swimme

ACKNOWLEDGMENTS

I WANT TO ACKNOWLEDGE all the deep self-hatred I took on as a child, along with fear and despair. Without these fierce teachers (along with my mentor Stephen Levine) I would never have found my way back to my heart.

I would also like to thank, from the deepest part of my heart, Devrah Bennett. She is my sister, my sidekick and my heart friend. Without her insight, technical knowledge and tireless support this book and this work would not be so available to the world.

ABOUT THE AUTHOR

MARY O'MALLEY is a speaker, author, group facilitator, and counselor in private practice in Kirkland, Washington. For more than thirty years, she has explored and practiced the art of being truly present for life. Her inspired and transformative approach to being with life, no matter what is happening, offers a way to replace fear, hopelessness and struggle with ease, wellbeing and joy. Through her organization, Awakening, she invites others into clarity, compassion, and trust. She offers an invitation to live from the place in which the impossible becomes possible and our hearts soar with the joy of being alive.

Mary offers online courses, audio CDs, four other books, engagements, retreats, workshops along with zoom, phone and in-person counseling and groups. For more, please visit maryomalley.com.

PRAISE FOR
MARY O'MALLEY'S BOOKS

Belonging to Life: The Journey of Awakening

Written with great love and compassion, *Belonging to Life* is a treasure of practical wisdom and profound insights, all point to one essential Truth: how to awaken into the present-moment awareness and live in acceptance of what is. Thank you, Mary, for your contribution to the evolution of human consciousness.

ECKHART TOLLE
Author of *The Power of Now*

I consider Mary O'Malley to be one of the most extraordinary teachers of our time. No one is more adept at showing us how to turn life's most difficult moments into life's greatest gifts. Her deep compassion, uncommon awareness, and crystal clear insight make anything she writes a treasure. This book can change your life for the better, forever.

NEALE DONALD WALSH
Author of *Conversations With God*

Belonging to Life is a gift to the world. Through story and metaphor, Mary invites her readers to move into the most challenging places of their lives. Easily and gently, she guides her readers into a place of curiosity and fascination, connecting them with themselves and with all of life.

REV. DEBORAH OLIVE
Sr. Minister, Unity of Olympia

Mary's voice is the clear and profound voice of an individual who has walked through the darkest of times and learned how to transmute the pain and wounding into precious treasure. Her words are her practice—she writes what she lives, honestly and authentically.

LINDA A. MORROW SPENCER
Sr. Minister, Unity of Santa Barbara

The Gift of Our Compulsions

Ancient wisdom tells us that the best solution to a problem is sometimes to relax into it rather than struggle and fight. This is the essential insight Mary O'Malley brings to the challenges of compulsive behaviors. As she explains, this involves the cultivation of compassion, forgiveness, and curiosity. Our culture, besotted with the desire for dominance and control, deeply needs this message.

LARRY DOSSEY, MD
Author of *Healing Words,
Reinventing Medicine,* and *Healing Beyond the Body*

Finally, a conscious, loving, and insightful way to understand and deal with our compulsions. Mary O'Malley has penetrated to the heart of healing behaviors that many of us find overwhelming. This book takes compulsion therapy to a whole new level.

ALAN COHEN
Author of *Mr. Everit's Secret*

Allow this book to be a companion and compassionate guide on your journey of awakening and to help you discover the perfection that is always already here, in the depth of the present moment, regardless of what is happening.

ECKHART TOLLE
Author of *The Power of Now*

The Magical Forest of Aliveness: A Tale of Awakening

Be careful! After reading this little story you may be out of your mind. In fact, with any luck you will be. Here is a wonderful piece of wisdom, sent, it would seem, from life itself TO life itself, and meant for every child and adult who picks up this book. A marvelous tale about the "stuff no one ever told us," but that would have changed our lives if they had, this small volume is bound to be among the treasured literature of every household into which it is introduced—which I hope will be many.

NEALE DONALD WALSH
Author of *Conversations With God*

What's In the Way IS the Way

"These teachings open you to mystery; they bring freedom, joy, and ease."

JACK KORNFIELD
Author of *A Path with Heart*

"Buddha said you could look the whole world over and never find anyone more deserving of love than yourself. Mary O'Malley awakens us again and again to the startling wonder of what lies beyond our workable hindrances, the liberation of our luminous nature."

STEPHEN LEVINE
Author of *A Year to Live*

"This is the most no-nonsense, grounded, accessible spirituality you will ever come across. I love Mary's teachings. They are simple and practical yet awesomely profound, and offer hope to those in even the darkest places. Her message is medicine for the world."

JEFF FOSTER
Author of *The Deepest Acceptance*

"This beautiful book is filled with heart wisdom. Mary O'Malley's teachings are simple, deep, and profoundly transforming . . . they will guide you in letting go and trusting life."

TARA BRACH, PHD
Author of *Radical Acceptance*

"Mary O'Malley is a genuine master, a sensible, plain-speaking exemplar of spiritual awakening and illuminated guidance. Every word in this book rings true. I loved it."

MARK MATOUSEK
Author of *When You're Falling, Dive*

"

In a world where we are pathologically encouraged to dismiss aspects of our authentic experience, this book is deeply welcome. With beautiful hearticulation, Mary O'Malley invites us to give voice to that which has been buried, illuminating pathways for transformation that are desperately needed in this mad world. An invitation to presence. An invitation to inclusivity. The wholly holy. This book comforts me."

JEFF BROWN
Author of *Soulshaping*

"Mary O'Malley's book shares meaningful information and wisdom. I know from my experience that she speaks the truth, and her guidance can make a significant difference in how we manage our journey through life."

BERNIE SIEGEL, MD
Author of Love, *Medicine and Miracles*

"Down-to-earth and joyful! Mary's words offer a healing path for all who wish to travel away from self-limiting views toward freedom of heart."

SHARON SALZBERG
Cofounder of the Insight Meditation Society
and author of *Real Happiness*

"Awakening is powerful medicine. A book to live with, learn from, and treasure."

CHRISTIANE NORTHRUP, MD, OB/GYN
Physician and author of *Women's Bodies, Women's Wisdom*

.

Printed by Amazon Italia Logistica S.r.l.
Torrazza Piemonte (TO), Italy